NOTE TO PARENTS

This beautifully illustrated book includes a selection of original prayers, each one inspired by a separate line from The Lord's Prayer. Each prayer is simple yet thoughtful and children will easily be able to relate the words to their own lives.

The Lord's Prayer

with original prayers by Marjorie Newman
illustrated by Dianne Stuchbury

Copyright © 1990 World International Publishing Limited.
All rights reserved.
Published in Great Britain by World International Publishing Limited,
An Egmont Company, Egmont House,
P.O. Box 111, Great Ducie Street,
Manchester M60 3BL.
Printed in DDR.
ISBN 0 7235 4470 0

A CIP catalogue record for this book is available from the British Library

Jesus taught us this special prayer.

Matthew 6: 9-13

Our Father, who art in Heaven,
Hallowed be Thy name.
Thy kingdom come,
Thy will be done
On earth, as it is in Heaven.
Give us this day our daily bread.
And forgive us our trespasses
As we forgive those who
    trespass against us.
And lead us not into temptation,
    but deliver us from evil.
For Thine is the kingdom, the
    power and the glory,
For ever and ever,
Amen.

OUR FATHER, WHO ART IN HEAVEN,

You are our loving Father, God.
You care for us each day.
You are in Heaven – yet close enough
To hear us when we pray.

HALLOWED BE THY NAME.

Your name is very special, God.
Help us to keep it so.
To never use it carelessly
As through our lives we go.

THY KINGDOM COME,
THY WILL BE DONE ON EARTH,

Please help us to do as *You* say, God.
Please help us to make You our King.
Then all of this earth will be happy,
And all of its people will sing!

AS IT IS IN HEAVEN.

Heaven is a lovely place
Where everyone is glad
For there, God's plans are carried out;
And no-one there is sad.

Give us this day our daily bread.

Please give to us today, O God,
The food You know we need –
Good things to eat, good things to see,
And good books we can read.
And help us too, O God, to share
The harvests that You give
So people everywhere will have
Enough to let them live.

AND FORGIVE US OUR TRESPASSES

Our Father God, we often do
Things that we know are wrong.
Please help us to be sorry, God.
Forgive us. Make us strong.

AS WE FORGIVE THOSE WHO TRESPASS AGAINST US.

Help us to be forgiving, God,
When people are unkind.
As soon as they are sorry, we
Will say – "Yes. Never mind."
If we forgive each other, God,
You can forgive us, too.
If we *won't* say "It's all right now,"
Then neither, God, can You.

And lead us not into temptation,

We ask You, God our Father,
To help us keep away
From all that makes us want to do
Wrong things, in work or play.

BUT DELIVER US FROM EVIL.

Evil can harm us, Father God,
There are dangers all around.
But You are strong to protect us, God.
Please keep us safe and sound.

For Thine is the kingdom,
the power and the glory,

Yours is the Kingdom of Love, God.
Your glory shines like a flame.
Your power is as great as the mighty wind.
All praise to Your holy name!

FOR EVER AND EVER,
AMEN.

Today, tomorrow, and yesterday.
This year, and next year too.
For ever and ever, You *are*, O God.
Our Father – we praise You!